TYRANNOSAURUS REX

by Bradley Cole

Cody Koala

An Imprint of Pop!
popbooksonline.com

abdobooks.com
Published by Pop!, a division of ABDO, PO Box 398166, Minneapolis, Minnesota 55439.

Printed in the United States of America, North Mankato, Minnesota

082018
012019

THIS BOOK CONTAINS RECYCLED MATERIALS

Cover Photo: iStockphoto
Interior Photos: iStockphoto, 1, 20; Mark Hallett Paleoart/Science Source, 5; Shutterstock Images, 7, 9, 10, 13; Mark Garlick/Science Source, 8; Francois Gohier/Science Source, 11; Science Picture Co/Science Source, 15; David R. Frazier/Science Source, 17 (top); Volker Steger/Science Source, 17 (bottom left); Richard T. Nowitz/Science Source, 17 (bottom right); The Natural History Museum, London/Science Source, 18

Editor: Meg Gaertner
Series Designer: Laura Mitchell

Library of Congress Control Number: 2018949754

Publisher's Cataloging-in-Publication Data
Names: Cole, Bradley, author.
Title: Tyrannosaurus rex / by Bradley Cole.
Description: Minneapolis, Minnesota : Pop!, 2019 | Series: Dinosaurs | Includes online resources and index.
Identifiers: ISBN 9781532161834 (lib. bdg.) | ISBN 9781641855549 (pbk) | ISBN 9781532162893 (ebook)
Subjects: LCSH: Tyrannosaurus rex--Juvenile literature. | Dinosaurs--Juvenile literature. | Extinct animals--Juvenile literature.
Classification: DDC 567.912--dc23

Hello! My name is

Cody Koala

Pop open this book and you'll find QR codes like this one, loaded with information, so you can learn even more!

Scan this code* and others like it while you read, or visit the website below to make this book pop.

popbooksonline.com/tyrannosaurus-rex

*Scanning QR codes requires a web-enabled smart device with a QR code reader app and a camera.

Table of Contents

Chapter 1

King of Lizards

Tyrannosaurus rex was a meat-eating dinosaur. Its name means “king of the tyrant lizards.” It lived about 68 million years ago.

The dinosaur’s name is often shortened to T. rex.

Watch a video here!

Chapter 2

Giant Predator

T. rex was a giant **predator**. It was about as long as a school bus. It could be as tall as a two-story building.

Learn more here!

T. rex ran on two strong legs. It had a powerful tail.

T. rex could reach speeds of 10 to 25 miles per hour.

It also had tiny arms.
Each arm had two fingers.
Scientists do not know why
the arms were so small.

T. rex had 60 pointy teeth for tearing meat. It had a strong bite.

The largest T. rex tooth found was as long as a foot.

T. rex could crush bones. It could eat 500 pounds of meat in one bite.

T. rex had a strong, thick neck. The dinosaur grabbed **prey** with its teeth. It pulled its head back to rip the prey apart.

strong tail
large teeth
tiny arms
strong legs

Chapter 3

Big Brain

Scientists think T. rex had a large **brain**. The dinosaur had a strong sense of smell. It used this sense to find prey. It also looked for dead animals to eat.

Learn more here!

Chapter 4

Fossils

Scientists found T. rex **fossils** in North America. The fossils were found in river valleys. **Paleontologists** learn a lot about the dinosaur from these fossils.

Complete an activity here!

an old idea of what T. rex looked like

Scientists used to think T. rex stood tall and dragged its tail. Now they think it leaned forward. It used its tail for **balance**.

Scientists found a fossil of the dinosaur's skin. It was scaly like a lizard's. But some scientists think T. rex **evolved** from dinosaurs with feathers.

Making Connections

Text-to-Self

Have you ever seen a dinosaur fossil in a museum? If yes, what did you think of it? If no, would you want to? Why or why not?

Text-to-Text

Have you read other books about dinosaurs? How did those dinosaurs compare to T. rex?

Text-to-World

T. rex used its sense of smell to find dead prey to eat. What other animals eat animals that are already dead?

Glossary

balance – the ability to remain standing and steady.

brain – the part of an animal used for thinking and memory.

evolved – gradually changed or grew over time.

fossil – the remains of a plant or an animal from a long time ago.

paleontologist – a scientist who studies the remains of animals from long ago.

predator – an animal that hunts other animals.

prey – an animal that is hunted by other animals.

Index

Online Resources

popbooksonline.com

Thanks for reading this Cody Koala book!

Scan this code* and others like it in this book, or visit the website below to make this book pop!

popbooksonline.com/tyrannosaurus-rex

*Scanning QR codes requires a web-enabled smart device with a QR code reader app and a camera.